30 Weeks of Prayer

Money Mindset

J.J. Thomas

First Published by Winged Publishing
Copyright © 2018

Scripture quotations are taken from the Holy Bible, New Living Translation, copyright ©1996, 2004, 2007, 2013, 2015 by Tyndale House Foundation. Used by permission of Tyndale House Publishers, Inc., Carol Stream, Illinois 60188. All rights reserved.

Edited and Formatted by Elizabeth Brighton Editing Services

Cover Design by Winged Publishing.
Stock Photo Found on canstockphoto.com
© Can Stock Photo Inc.

Table of Contents

Budgeting

Week 1: The one and only budgeting tip God promises will fill your storehouses!

Week 2: #1 clever thing advanced budgeters do differently

Managing Debt

Week 3: Top 3 insightful questions to ask when you're drowning in debt

Week 4: How one life-changing experience will help you climb out of debt

Breaking Locked Doors

Week 5: How to activate your incredible power to succeed (and it's not what you think!)

Week 6: Warning! Your words may be destroying your life

Week 7: Are your prayers blocked? God has the solution

Dealing with Self-Sabotage

Week 8: 1 brutally honest fact those who love spending money should know

Week 9: Is your job sucking your life away? Here's how to fix it

Week 10: Warning! You may be sabotaging your own success!

Week 11: 3 surprising things you didn't know about humility and what you can get from it

Week 12: Wearing yourself thin? Here's how to fix it

Week 13: 2 amazing people who can change your life

Week 14: Struggling to keep up with the Joneses? Here's how to fix it

Week 15: Do get-rich-quick schemes ever work? Here's what God says about it

Financial Planning

Week 16: Why thoughtful preparation can build your dream home

Week 17: Why trusting God's plans will get you where you need to be

Week 18: Why your financial plans may be crippling your future

Week 19: The ultimate guide to mastering your financial plans

Week 20: How to plan for prosperity – God's life-changing way

Investing

Week 21: The #1 daring strategy for getting rich without losing your soul

Week 22: Solomon's brazen guide to investing in today's world

Living Prosperously

Week 23: 2 things only the truly prosperous understand about finding enduring riches

Week 24: How to pray like a warrior and find God's enduring answers to your problems

Week 25: Crying to God for help? Here's God's incredible promise to you

Week 26: 1 daring promise to remember when life gets tough

Week 27: Do you have enough faith to move mountains? Here's what your Heavenly Father says about it

Week 28: The ultimate key to answered prayer

Week 29: How to be a fearless prayer warrior after God's own heart

Week 30: How to prioritize like a boss and why money will never really matter

God's Insider Guide to

Understanding Your Finances

> But if any of you lacks wisdom, let him ask of God,
>
> who gives to all generously and without reproach,
>
> and it will be given to him
>
> **James 1:5 NLT**

Newlyweds, my husband and I were jobless, penniless, homeless, and drowning in debt. Pregnant with our first child, we lived with my in-laws for more than a year while my husband, a college graduate who couldn't find a job in his field, worked temp factory jobs at minimum wage.

It was humiliating. Frustrating. Desperate. Hopeless.

Eventually, I found a job, we rented a small house, and my husband became stay-at-home dad while Baby Girl #2 was on the way. Single income family, we lived paycheck to paycheck, struggling to make ends meet. Usually, our checking account was overdrawn while our savings was always empty. We had to pray we would have enough food and gas to make it to the next paycheck.

We bought an old house in a poor neighborhood, and soon after, Baby #3 came along. When I was laid off about a year later, we lost our home before I could find another job.

In fifteen years, I climbed the corporate ladder: from Software Test Analyst to Sr. Software Test Engineer. I more than doubled my income, but then we also had more expenses: a house, a leased car, dance lessons and music lessons for the kids, higher utility bills …

Still living paycheck to paycheck, I realized more money does not solve my money problems. What I really need is wisdom.

What I need is God's mindset on how to use my money.

Thus I began to study what the Bible says about money and money management. This prayer journal is centered on the thirty verses God used to enlighten me.

From these verses, I learned that true financial freedom consists of four things:

- Being debt free so I don't have excess expenses
- Choosing my job based on what I love to do rather than the income it provides
- Having enough time and money to give generously, to save wisely, to have some fun while still covering my responsibilities
- No longer worrying because I know God holds us in his hands

The secrets to managing your finances are available to you too. The Bible is full of answers to your questions: how to budget, set your priorities, overcome debt, invest for your future, and root out your personal sabotages.

To open these secrets to you, all you have to do is ask God for his wisdom.

What you need to do each week:

Each week will focus on a different scripture related to your finances. Follow these simple steps to make the most of the 30 weeks of prayer:

1. Read the weekly scripture verse and write it down in the Bible version that speaks the most to you.

2. Fill in your personal thoughts about the weekly scripture.

3. Each day, fill in the sections for the daily prayer:

    ➢ **Day One: Prayer of Cleansing**
    Purify your heart and mind to allow God's word to sink in

    ➢ **Day Two: Prayer of Forgiveness**
    Forgive others to make way for new blessings in your life

    ➢ **Day Three: Prayer of Requests**
    Make your requests known to the Lord

    ➢ **Day Four: Quiet Listening**
    Take the time to hear God's words to you because he always asks us to participate in making miracles happen

    ➢ **Day Five: Prayer of Promises**
    Stand firm on God's promises

    ➢ **Day Six: Words of Power**
    Speak God's promises over your finances because words have power

    ➢ **Day Seven: Prayer of Thanksgiving**
    Thank God for his blessings, even if you can't see them yet because gratitude blesses God's heart

4. Follow through with obedience in what God is calling you to do.

Helpful hints:

Here are a few things to keep in mind each day:

1. **Ask God to give you the right prayers.**
   I purposefully left as many open-ended questions and spaces to give the Holy Spirit room to work through you.

2. **Seek God to be your answer.**
   In God, we trust. Not in money or brains or jobs or dreams. Even while we are looking inward, in order to align ourselves to God's word, we cannot let that cloud our sight from the one and only Answer to all our problems.

   Jesus began a good work in us and he will finish it (Philippians 1:6). The Holy Spirit convicts rather than condemns us by showing us how much Jesus loved us and died for us even when we were still sinners (Romans 5:8). During the next 30 weeks, you will be looking in the mirror and will see your sin, your unforgiveness, and your self-sabotage.

   Don't take on the burden of trying to fix yourself. Repent, forgive, listen and obey, speak powerful words, and let God take care of the rest.

3. **Actively listen to God's directions over your situation.**
   Throughout both the Old and New Testament, God frequently asked people to participate in their own miracles. Abraham left his home and family – his comfort zone – and the children of Israel marched around a city. One leper washed in the Jordan River (2 Kings 5), and a woman poured oil into borrowed pots to save her children from slavery.

4. **Control your tongue.**
   God created the world with his voice, and the Bible says his Word goes out and accomplishes what he planned (Isaiah 55:11). Remember: we were made in his image. We too have the power to speak both blessings and curses over our lives (Proverbs 18:21, James 3:10).

Join the 30 Weeks of Prayer Challenge: Money Mindset

The prayer challenge is a weekly email that is the companion of this personal prayer journal.

When you sign up for the weekly Challenge, you will have access to the following resources:

- Budget
- Expense Tracking
- Debt Payoff Plan
- Worksheets and more

You can sign up here: https://mailchi.mp/49d7deb9f7bc/30weeksofprayer

Or use this QR code to sign up from your phone:

The one and
only budgeting
tip God
promises will
fill your
storehouses!

~ Proverbs 3:9-10

Hey friend ~

When the bills pile up and you have to choose between tithe and putting food on the table, what are you going to pick?

Money that somehow always slips through your fingers? Or the one who fed the 5,000 with a few loaves of bread and some small fish, who turned water into wine, who provided manna in the wilderness?

God wants to know you *trust* him enough to give to him first and foremost while everything else – the mortgage, credit cards, utilities, entertainment, your wish list, even your dreams – comes second.

He wants to know you *love* him more than anything else.

Reflection

What is God speaking to you about this week's verse?

_____

_____

_____

_____

_____

_____

_____

_____

_____

_____

_____

What actions is God asking of you?

☐ _____

☐ _____

☐ _____

☐ _____

☐ _____

Prayer of Cleansing

Day One: _____/_____/_____

Lord, I love you ...

_____

_____

Lord, I am sorry for ...

_____

_____

_____

Lord, please forgive me. Help me to ...

_____

_____

Lord, thank you for ...

_____

_____

_____

_____

Prayer of Forgiveness

Day Two: _____/_____/_____

Lord, I forgive _____

Lord, I love them despite everything. Please bless them ...

_____

_____

_____

_____

Lord, thank you for teaching me ...

_____

_____

_____

Lord, I am sorry for my part in the situation ...

_____

_____

_____

_____

Prayer of Requests

Day Three: _____/_____/_____

Lord, I need a miracle ...

_____

_____

_____

_____

_____

_____

_____

_____

_____

_____

_____

_____

_____

_____

_____

Quiet Listening

Day Four: _____/_____/_____

> Listen to God's quiet voice. What is he speaking to you?

_____

_____

_____

_____

_____

_____

_____

_____

_____

_____

> What do you need to do to be obedient to his voice?

_____

_____

_____

_____

Words of Promise

Day Five: _____/_____/_____

What has God promised you?

_____

_____

_____

_____

_____

_____

_____

_____

_____

_____

What does God want you to do to be a part of his promise?

_____

_____

_____

_____

Words of Power

Day Six: _____/_____/_____

God's promises are strong and sure. His Word tells me ...

_____

_____

_____

_____

_____

_____

_____

_____

_____

_____

_____

_____

_____

Prayer of Thanksgiving

Day Seven: _____/_____/_____

List five things you are thankful for this week:

1. _____

2. _____

3. _____

4. _____

5. _____

What miracle, great or small, did God give you this week?

_____

_____

_____

_____

_____

Thank you, Lord, for all you have done for me this week ...

_____

_____

_____

_____

#1 clever thing
advanced
budgeters do
differently

_____

_____

_____

_____

_____

_____

~ Proverbs 23:4–5

Hey friend ~

Took me a long time to realize FLOCKS = RESOURCES. Take care of your resources so they can take care of you.

Your house, your body, your garden if you have one, your car (because it gets you to work), home repair and maintenance – these are all things a smart budgeter knows to prioritize above other expenses.

Priority #1 = God

Priority #2 = Resources and their Maintenance

I created a budget & expense tracker worksheet, which you can get as part of the Prayer Challenge email for week 2.

Reflection

What is God speaking to you about this week's verse?

_____

_____

_____

_____

_____

_____

_____

_____

_____

_____

What actions is God asking of you?

☐ _____

☐ _____

☐ _____

☐ _____

☐ _____

Prayer of Cleansing

Day One: _____/_____/_____

Lord, I love you ...

_____

_____

_____

Lord, I am sorry for ...

_____

_____

_____

_____

Lord, please forgive me. Help me to ...

_____

_____

Lord, thank you for ...

_____

_____

_____

_____

Prayer of Forgiveness

Day Two: _____/_____/_____

Lord, I forgive _____

Lord, I love them despite everything. Please bless them ...

_____

_____

_____

_____

Lord, thank you for teaching me ...

_____

_____

_____

_____

Lord, I am sorry for my part in the situation ...

_____

_____

_____

_____

Prayer of Requests

Day Three: _____/_____/_____

Lord, I need a miracle ...

_____

_____

_____

_____

_____

_____

_____

_____

_____

_____

_____

_____

_____

_____

_____

Quiet Listening

Day Four: _____/_____/_____

_____

_____

_____

_____

_____

_____

_____

_____

_____

_____

What do you need to do to be obedient to his voice?

_____

_____

_____

_____

Words of Promise

Day Five: _____/_____/_____

What has God promised you?

_____

_____

_____

_____

_____

_____

_____

_____

_____

_____

What does God want you to do to be a part of his promise?

_____

_____

_____

_____

Words of Power

Day Six: _____ / _____ / _____

| God's promises are strong and sure. His Word tells me ... |

_____

_____

_____

_____

_____

_____

_____

_____

_____

_____

_____

_____

_____

_____

_____

Prayer of Thanksgiving

Day Seven: _____/_____/_____

List five things you are thankful for this week:

1. _____

2. _____

3. _____

4. _____

5. _____

What miracle, great or small, did God give you this week?

_____

_____

_____

_____

_____

Thank you, Lord, for all you have done for me this week ...

_____

_____

_____

_____

Week 3

Top 3 insightful questions to ask when you're drowning in debt

_____

_____

_____

_____

_____

_____

~ Proverbs 22:7

Hey friend ~

I have some words for you: **_Debt isn't God's plan for you!_**

He doesn't want you chained down, frustrated and discouraged, struggling only to barely survive week to week. That's what debt does to you.

Time to tackle that debt and kick it to the curb. 3 questions to ask yourself:

- Which debt can be paid off the fastest?
- Which debt has the highest interest rate?
- What can you do to bring in some extra income?

In this week's Prayer Challenge email, I shared a debt plan to help you get started. Ask God to help you come up with the right plan for you.

Reflection

What is God speaking to you about this week's verse?

_____

_____

_____

_____

_____

_____

_____

_____

_____

_____

_____

What actions is God asking of you?

☐ _____

☐ _____

☐ _____

☐ _____

☐ _____

Prayer of Cleansing

Day One: _____/_____/_____

Lord, I love you ...

_____

_____

_____

Lord, I am sorry for ...

_____

_____

_____

Lord, please forgive me. Help me to ...

_____

_____

Lord, thank you for ...

_____

_____

_____

_____

Prayer of Forgiveness

Day Two: _____/_____/_____

Lord, I forgive _____

Lord, I love them despite everything. Please bless them ...

_____

_____

_____

Lord, thank you for teaching me ...

_____

_____

_____

Lord, I am sorry for my part in the situation ...

_____

_____

_____

Prayer of Requests

Day Three: _____ / _____ / _____

Lord, I need a miracle ...

_____

_____

_____

_____

_____

_____

_____

_____

_____

_____

_____

_____

_____

_____

Quiet Listening

Day Four: _____/_____/_____

Listen to God's quiet voice. What is he speaking to you?

_____

_____

_____

_____

_____

_____

_____

_____

_____

What do you need to do to be obedient to his voice?

_____

_____

_____

Words of Promise

Day Five: _____/_____/_____

What has God promised you?

_____

_____

_____

_____

_____

_____

_____

_____

_____

_____

What does God want you to do to be a part of his promise?

_____

_____

_____

_____

Words of Power

Day Six: _____ / _____ / _____

God's promises are strong and sure. His Word tells me ...

_____

_____

_____

_____

_____

_____

_____

_____

_____

_____

_____

_____

_____

_____

_____

Prayer of Thanksgiving

Day Seven: _____/_____/_____

List five things you are thankful for this week:

1. _____

2. _____

3. _____

4. _____

5. _____

What miracle, great or small, did God give you this week?

_____

_____

_____

_____

_____

Thank you, Lord, for all you have done for me this week ...

_____

_____

_____

Week 4

How one life-changing experience will help you climb out of debt

_____

_____

_____

_____

_____

_____

~ Matthew 6:12

Hey friend ~

Just as debt chains our finances, so unforgiveness chains our souls.

In my book **Dream Catcher**, I told the story of how forgiveness set me free from the chains of depression. Someone's biting words wounded me so deeply, I poured over them until each word was ingrained in my memory. It became the focus of my life.

… that is, until I forgave her. God set both my heart and soul free.

The physical state of our lives often reflects the spiritual. Baggage we carry, like debt, clutter, or poverty, can sometimes indicate things we need to work on inside.

A forgiveness worksheet is available in this week's Prayer Challenge email, so please take a moment to go through it.

Reflection

What is God speaking to you about this week's verse?

_____

_____

_____

_____

_____

_____

_____

_____

_____

_____

What actions is God asking of you?

☐ _____

☐ _____

☐ _____

☐ _____

☐ _____

Prayer of Cleansing

Day One: _____/_____/_____

Lord, I love you ...

_____

_____

Lord, I am sorry for ...

_____

_____

_____

Lord, please forgive me. Help me to ...

_____

_____

Lord, thank you for ...

_____

_____

_____

_____

Prayer of Forgiveness

Day Two: _____/_____/_____

Lord, I forgive _____

Lord, I love them despite everything. Please bless them ...

_____

_____

_____

Lord, thank you for teaching me ...

_____

_____

_____

Lord, I am sorry for my part in the situation ...

_____

_____

_____

Prayer of Requests

Day Three: _____ / _____ / _____

Lord, I need a miracle ...

_____

_____

_____

_____

_____

_____

_____

_____

_____

_____

_____

_____

_____

_____

_____

Quiet Listening

Day Four: _____/_____/_____

Listen to God's quiet voice. What is he speaking to you?

_____

_____

_____

_____

_____

_____

_____

_____

_____

_____

What do you need to do to be obedient to his voice?

_____

_____

_____

_____

Words of Promise

Day Five: _____/_____/_____

What has God promised you?

_____

_____

_____

_____

_____

_____

_____

_____

_____

_____

What does God want you to do to be a part of his promise?

_____

_____

_____

_____

Words of Power

Day Six: _____/_____/_____

> God's promises are strong and sure. His Word tells me ...

_____

_____

_____

_____

_____

_____

_____

_____

_____

_____

_____

_____

_____

_____

Prayer of Thanksgiving

Day Seven: _____/_____/_____

List five things you are thankful for this week:

1. _____

2. _____

3. _____

4. _____

5. _____

What miracle, great or small, did God give you this week?

_____

_____

_____

_____

_____

Thank you, Lord, for all you have done for me this week ...

_____

_____

_____

_____

How to activate your incredible power to succeed (and it's not what you think!)

~ Proverbs 13:2-3

A few words from Joy ...

Hey friend ~

Words have power.

Don't you know you were made in the image of the Almighty Creator?
He spoke the world into existence! And like him, power is in your
tongue, the power to create life and death (Proverbs 18:21).

What do your words say about your finances? What fruit are you
producing with your lips?

Time to start creating something good and powerful with your words.
Time to start exercising your faith and speaking prophetically about your
life, your money, and your opportunities.

Reflection

What is God speaking to you about this week's verse?

_____

_____

_____

_____

_____

_____

_____

_____

_____

_____

_____

What actions is God asking of you?

☐ _____

☐ _____

☐ _____

☐ _____

☐ _____

Prayer of Cleansing

Day One: _____/_____/_____

Lord, I love you ...

_____

_____

Lord, I am sorry for ...

_____

_____

_____

Lord, please forgive me. Help me to ...

_____

_____

Lord, thank you for ...

_____

_____

_____

_____

Prayer of Forgiveness

Day Two: _____/_____/_____

Lord, I forgive _____

Lord, I love them despite everything. Please bless them ...

_____

_____

_____

_____

Lord, thank you for teaching me ...

_____

_____

_____

_____

Lord, I am sorry for my part in the situation ...

_____

_____

_____

_____

Prayer of Requests

Day Three: _____/_____/_____

Lord, I need a miracle ...

_____

_____

_____

_____

_____

_____

_____

_____

_____

_____

_____

_____

_____

_____

_____

_____

Quiet Listening

Day Four: _____/_____/_____

Listen to God's quiet voice. What is he speaking to you?

_____

_____

_____

_____

_____

_____

_____

_____

_____

_____

What do you need to do to be obedient to his voice?

_____

_____

_____

_____

Words of Promise

Day Five: _____/_____/_____

What has God promised you?

_____

_____

_____

_____

_____

_____

_____

_____

_____

_____

What does God want you to do to be a part of his promise?

_____

_____

_____

_____

Words of Power

Day Six: _____/_____/_____

God's promises are strong and sure. His Word tells me ...

_____

_____

_____

_____

_____

_____

_____

_____

_____

_____

_____

_____

_____

_____

Prayer of Thanksgiving

Day Seven: _____/_____/_____

List five things you are thankful for this week:

1. _____

2. _____

3. _____

4. _____

5. _____

What miracle, great or small, did God give you this week?

_____

_____

_____

_____

_____

Thank you, Lord, for all you have done for me this week ...

_____

_____

_____

_____

Week 6

Warning! Your words may be destroying your life

_____

_____

_____

_____

_____

_____

~ Proverbs 18:21

A few words from Joy ...

Hey friend ~

I need to repeat what I said last week: Words have power!

Someday, we – you and me both – will be judged for every idle word coming out of our mouths (Matthew 12:36).

When it comes to money, we say some terrible things, but none of those words reflect the awesome caring Provider who promised to take care of our needs.

Every time things went wrong while wandering the desert for forty years, the children of Israel griped and complained, wailing how God had abandoned them … despite all the previous miracles and blessings he gave them.

When things go wrong, what are the first words out of your mouth?

Next time, bite your tongue, hold it back, refuse to speak until you can say life-giving words. Better yet, find something you can be thankful for.

Reflection

What is God speaking to you about this week's verse?

_____

_____

_____

_____

_____

_____

_____

_____

_____

_____

_____

What actions is God asking of you?

☐ _____

☐ _____

☐ _____

☐ _____

☐ _____

Prayer of Cleansing

Day One: ____/____/_____

Lord, I love you ...

_____

_____

_____

Lord, I am sorry for ...

_____

_____

_____

Lord, please forgive me. Help me to ...

_____

_____

Lord, thank you for ...

_____

_____

_____

Prayer of Forgiveness

Day Two: _____ / _____ / _____

Lord, I forgive _____

Lord, I love them despite everything. Please bless them ...

_____

_____

_____

Lord, thank you for teaching me ...

_____

_____

_____

Lord, I am sorry for my part in the situation ...

_____

_____

_____

Prayer of Requests

Day Three: ____/____/_____

Lord, I need a miracle ...

_____

_____

_____

_____

_____

_____

_____

_____

_____

_____

_____

_____

_____

_____

_____

Quiet Listening

Day Four: _____/_____/_____

Listen to God's quiet voice. What is he speaking to you?

_____

_____

_____

_____

_____

_____

_____

_____

_____

_____

What do you need to do to be obedient to his voice?

_____

_____

_____

_____

Words of Promise

Day Five: _____/_____/_____

What has God promised you?

_____

_____

_____

_____

_____

_____

_____

_____

_____

_____

What does God want you to do to be a part of his promise?

_____

_____

_____

_____

Words of Power

Day Six: _____/_____/_____

God's promises are strong and sure. His Word tells me ...

_____

_____

_____

_____

_____

_____

_____

_____

_____

_____

_____

_____

_____

Prayer of Thanksgiving

Day Seven: _____/_____/_____

List five things you are thankful for this week:

1. _____

2. _____

3. _____

4. _____

5. _____

What miracle, great or small, did God give you this week?

_____

_____

_____

_____

Thank you, Lord, for all you have done for me this week ...

_____

_____

_____

Are your prayers blocked? God has the solution

_____

_____

_____

_____

_____

_____

~ James 4:2b-3

A few words from Joy ...

Hey friend ~

When we ask for God's intervention in our finances and nothing happens, it is because we need to become an active participant. Sometimes, we need to clear our motivations or rid ourselves of excess baggage.

In my book *Dream Catcher*, I shared my personal journey to catching my dreams. I learned intercessory prayer has a four step process:

- Confession and Repentance
- Forgiveness
- Listening and Obedience
- Prophetic Profession of Faith

Reflection

> What is God speaking to you about this week's verse?

_____

_____

_____

_____

_____

_____

_____

_____

_____

_____

_____

> What actions is God asking of you?

☐ _____

☐ _____

☐ _____

☐ _____

☐ _____

Prayer of Cleansing

Day One: _____/_____/_____

Lord, I love you ...

Lord, I am sorry for ...

Lord, please forgive me. Help me to ...

Lord, thank you for ...

Prayer of Forgiveness

Day Two: _____/_____/_____

Lord, I forgive _____

Lord, I love them despite everything. Please bless them ...

_____

_____

_____

Lord, thank you for teaching me ...

_____

_____

_____

Lord, I am sorry for my part in the situation ...

_____

_____

_____

Prayer of Requests

Day Three: _____/_____/_____

Lord, I need a miracle ...

_____

_____

_____

_____

_____

_____

_____

_____

_____

_____

_____

_____

_____

_____

Quiet Listening

Day Four: _____/_____/_____

_____

_____

_____

_____

_____

_____

_____

_____

_____

_____

What do you need to do to be obedient to his voice?

_____

_____

_____

_____

Words of Promise

Day Five: _____/_____/_____

What has God promised you?

_____

_____

_____

_____

_____

_____

_____

_____

_____

_____

What does God want you to do to be a part of his promise?

_____

_____

_____

_____

Words of Power

Day Six: _____/_____/_____

God's promises are strong and sure. His Word tells me ...

_____

_____

_____

_____

_____

_____

_____

_____

_____

_____

_____

_____

_____

_____

Prayer of Thanksgiving

Day Seven: _____ / _____ / _____

List five things you are thankful for this week:

1. _____

2. _____

3. _____

4. _____

5. _____

What miracle, great or small, did God give you this week?

_____

_____

_____

_____

_____

Thank you, Lord, for all you have done for me this week ...

_____

_____

_____

_____

1 brutally honest fact those who love spending money should know

~ Proverbs 21:17, 20

_____

_____

_____

_____

_____

_____

Hey friend ~

Spending money can be addictive. It fills a hole in our hearts – a hole that can only be truly filled with Jesus.

Over the years, my husband and I learned to make a wish list – one for the year with big purchases on it, another for the short term. A new couch – long term. The kids all need haircuts and new shoes – short term.

When money is available, we cross something off the list. When it's not, we wait. Sometimes, it takes a while to see the blessing fulfilled. Other times, things get put on the list that a few weeks later, we realize we don't need or even want.

God has always provided those things we truly wanted and needed. At the end of the year, we can count up all the blessings God provided and thank him for his goodness.

Reflection

What is God speaking to you about this week's verse?

_____

_____

_____

_____

_____

_____

_____

_____

_____

_____

What actions is God asking of you?

☐ _____

☐ _____

☐ _____

☐ _____

☐ _____

Prayer of Cleansing

Day One: _____/_____/_____

Lord, I love you ...

_____

_____

_____

Lord, I am sorry for ...

_____

_____

_____

Lord, please forgive me. Help me to ...

_____

_____

Lord, thank you for ...

_____

_____

_____

Prayer of Forgiveness

Day Two: _____/_____/_____

Lord, I forgive _____

Lord, I love them despite everything. Please bless them ...

_____

_____

_____

Lord, thank you for teaching me ...

_____

_____

_____

Lord, I am sorry for my part in the situation ...

_____

_____

_____

Prayer of Requests

Day Three: _____ / _____ / _____

Lord, I need a miracle ...

_____

_____

_____

_____

_____

_____

_____

_____

_____

_____

_____

_____

_____

_____

_____

_____

Quiet Listening

Day Four: _____/_____/_____

Listen to God's quiet voice. What is he speaking to you?

_____

_____

_____

_____

_____

_____

_____

_____

What do you need to do to be obedient to his voice?

_____

_____

_____

Words of Promise

Day Five: _____/_____/_____

What has God promised you?

_____

_____

_____

_____

_____

_____

_____

_____

_____

_____

What does God want you to do to be a part of his promise?

_____

_____

_____

_____

Words of Power

Day Six: _____/_____/_____

God's promises are strong and sure. His Word tells me ...

_____

_____

_____

_____

_____

_____

_____

_____

_____

_____

_____

_____

_____

Prayer of Thanksgiving

Day Seven: _____ / _____ / _____

List five things you are thankful for this week:

1. _____

2. _____

3. _____

4. _____

5. _____

What miracle, great or small, did God give you this week?

_____

_____

_____

_____

_____

Thank you, Lord, for all you have done for me this week ...

_____

_____

_____

_____

Is your job sucking your life away? Here's how to fix it

_____

_____

_____

_____

_____

_____

~ Proverbs 1:18–19

A few words from Joy ...

Hey friend ~

More money doesn't solve your money problems. If you are wasteful with money now, you'll be just as wasteful when you have more.

In the same way, a better job isn't going to make you feel more fulfilled.

The most important lesson you learn when starting your own business is that your business is not about making money but about fulfilling a greater purpose. **People are your greater purpose**, no matter what you do to make a living.

If you can fulfill this purpose – loving people, encouraging people, building them up, equipping them to do their jobs better, empowering them – then you will find joy in the most boring, painful, mundane job in existence.

Be faithful in this and trust the Lord for the rest.

Reflection

_____

_____

_____

_____

_____

_____

_____

_____

_____

_____

_____

What actions is God asking of you?

☐ _____

☐ _____

☐ _____

☐ _____

☐ _____

Prayer of Cleansing

Day One: _____ / _____ / _____

Lord, I love you ...

_____

_____

_____

Lord, I am sorry for ...

_____

_____

_____

Lord, please forgive me. Help me to ...

_____

_____

Lord, thank you for ...

_____

_____

_____

_____

Prayer of Forgiveness

Day Two: _____ / _____ / _____

| Lord, I forgive _____ |

| Lord, I love them despite everything. Please bless them ... |

_____

_____

_____

| Lord, thank you for teaching me ... |

_____

_____

_____

| Lord, I am sorry for my part in the situation ... |

_____

_____

_____

Prayer of Requests

Day Three: _____/_____/_____

Lord, I need a miracle ...

_____

_____

_____

_____

_____

_____

_____

_____

_____

_____

_____

_____

_____

_____

Quiet Listening

Day Four: _____/_____/_____

Listen to God's quiet voice. What is he speaking to you?

_____

_____

_____

_____

_____

_____

_____

_____

_____

_____

_____

What do you need to do to be obedient to his voice?

_____

_____

_____

_____

Words of Promise

Day Five: _____/_____/_____

What has God promised you?

_____

_____

_____

_____

_____

_____

_____

_____

_____

_____

_____

What does God want you to do to be a part of his promise?

_____

_____

_____

_____

Words of Power

Day Six: ____/____/_____

> God's promises are strong and sure. His Word tells me ...

_____

_____

_____

_____

_____

_____

_____

_____

_____

_____

_____

_____

_____

_____

Prayer of Thanksgiving

Day Seven: _____ / _____ / _____

List five things you are thankful for this week:

1. _____

2. _____

3. _____

4. _____

5. _____

What miracle, great or small, did God give you this week?

_____

_____

_____

_____

_____

Thank you, Lord, for all you have done for me this week ...

_____

_____

_____

_____

Week 10

Warning!
You may be sabotaging your own success!

~ Proverbs 6:9–11

A few words from Joy ...

Hey friend ~

This isn't just about having a job, working hard. It's about your follow-through.

Like prioritizing resource-related expenses over other bills, we need to prioritize our time and effort behind activities that help us save money. Planning your meals, making a grocery list, keeping your kitchen clean and ready for cooking – these activities help you save money on groceries and eating out.

Exercising and taking care of your body prevents future health issues and expenses. Maintaining your home takes effort but can improve your property value and possibly even its energy efficiency.

Think about your activities, how you prioritize your time, and submit it to the Lord.

Reflection

What is God speaking to you about this week's verse?

_____

_____

_____

_____

_____

_____

_____

_____

_____

_____

_____

What actions is God asking of you?

- ☐ _____
- ☐ _____
- ☐ _____
- ☐ _____
- ☐ _____

Prayer of Cleansing

Day One: _____ / _____ / _____

Lord, I love you ...

_____

_____

Lord, I am sorry for ...

_____

_____

_____

Lord, please forgive me. Help me to ...

_____

_____

Lord, thank you for ...

_____

_____

_____

_____

Prayer of Forgiveness

Day Two: _____/_____/_____

Lord, I forgive _____

Lord, I love them despite everything. Please bless them ...

_____

_____

_____

Lord, thank you for teaching me ...

_____

_____

_____

Lord, I am sorry for my part in the situation ...

_____

_____

_____

Prayer of Requests

Day Three: ____/____/_____

Lord, I need a miracle ...

_____

_____

_____

_____

_____

_____

_____

_____

_____

_____

_____

_____

_____

_____

_____

Quiet Listening

Day Four: _____/_____/_____

Listen to God's quiet voice. What is he speaking to you?

_____

_____

_____

_____

_____

_____

_____

_____

_____

What do you need to do to be obedient to his voice?

_____

_____

_____

_____

Words of Promise

Day Five: _____/_____/_____

What has God promised you?

_____

_____

_____

_____

_____

_____

_____

_____

_____

What does God want you to do to be a part of his promise?

_____

_____

_____

_____

Words of Power

Day Six: _____/_____/_____

God's promises are strong and sure. His Word tells me ...

_____

_____

_____

_____

_____

_____

_____

_____

_____

_____

_____

_____

_____

_____

_____

_____

Prayer of Thanksgiving

Day Seven: _____/_____/_____

List five things you are thankful for this week:

1. _____

2. _____

3. _____

4. _____

5. _____

What miracle, great or small, did God give you this week?

_____

_____

_____

_____

_____

Thank you, Lord, for all you have done for me this week ...

_____

_____

_____

_____

Week 11

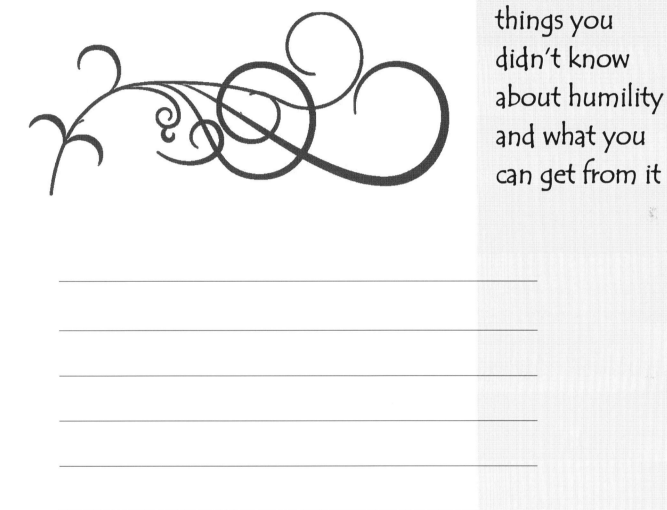

3 surprising
things you
didn't know
about humility
and what you
can get from it

_____

_____

_____

_____

_____

_____

_____

~ Proverbs 22:4

Hey friend ~

Humility is a combination of awe and trust in the Lord, and it comes from an understanding of how big and amazing God really is. Once you know how big he is, you can see how small you really are.

C.S. Lewis defined humility as *knowing yourself*.

Imagine if you could honestly speak equally about your strengths and weaknesses. What would it be like if you could accept and even love yourself exactly the way you are – your chubby spots, your failures, the color of your hair, the ridiculous smile you see in a picture of you?

When you can celebrate the accomplishments of others with the same joy and excitement as you celebrate your own, and vice versa, then you have humility.

Your reward is 3 things: riches, honor, and a long life.

Reflection

What is God speaking to you about this week's verse?

_____

_____

_____

_____

_____

_____

_____

_____

_____

_____

What actions is God asking of you?

- ☐ _____
- ☐ _____
- ☐ _____
- ☐ _____
- ☐ _____

Prayer of Cleansing

Day One: _____/_____/_____

Lord, I love you ...

_____

_____

_____

Lord, I am sorry for ...

_____

_____

_____

_____

Lord, please forgive me. Help me to ...

_____

_____

Lord, thank you for ...

_____

_____

_____

_____

Prayer of Forgiveness

Day Two: _____/_____/_____

Lord, I forgive _____

Lord, I love them despite everything. Please bless them ...

_____

_____

_____

Lord, thank you for teaching me ...

_____

_____

_____

Lord, I am sorry for my part in the situation ...

_____

_____

_____

Prayer of Requests

Day Three: _____ / _____ / _____

Lord, I need a miracle ...

_____

_____

_____

_____

_____

_____

_____

_____

_____

_____

_____

_____

_____

_____

Quiet Listening

Day Four: _____/_____/_____

Listen to God's quiet voice. What is he speaking to you?

_____

_____

_____

_____

_____

_____

_____

_____

_____

What do you need to do to be obedient to his voice?

_____

_____

_____

Words of Promise

Day Five: _____/_____/_____

What has God promised you?

_____

_____

_____

_____

_____

_____

_____

_____

_____

_____

What does God want you to do to be a part of his promise?

_____

_____

_____

_____

Words of Power

Day Six: _____ / _____ / _____

God's promises are strong and sure. His Word tells me ...

_____

_____

_____

_____

_____

_____

_____

_____

_____

_____

_____

_____

_____

_____

Prayer of Thanksgiving

Day Seven: _____/_____/_____

List five things you are thankful for this week:

1. _____

2. _____

3. _____

4. _____

5. _____

What miracle, great or small, did God give you this week?

_____

_____

_____

_____

_____

Thank you, Lord, for all you have done for me this week ...

_____

_____

_____

Week 12

Wearing yourself thin? Here's how to fix it

~ Proverbs 23:4–5

A few words from Joy ...

Hey friend ~

Money doesn't buy happiness. Money is only a tool, and without wisdom, it's an ineffective one at that.

Contentment brings us peace and happiness.

Can you be content with where you are right now, on your journey? Can you be proud of your accomplishments instead of berating yourself for where you've failed? Can you let go of your next goal, for even a short while, and take a moment to *live*, to just be?

When was the last time you took time to play, dance, sing, laugh?

Reflection

_____

_____

_____

_____

_____

_____

_____

_____

_____

_____

What actions is God asking of you?

☐ _____

☐ _____

☐ _____

☐ _____

☐ _____

Prayer of Cleansing

Day One: _____ / _____ / _____

Lord, I love you ...

_____

_____

Lord, I am sorry for ...

_____

_____

_____

Lord, please forgive me. Help me to ...

_____

_____

Lord, thank you for ...

_____

_____

_____

Prayer of Forgiveness

Day Two: _____/_____/_____

Lord, I forgive _____

Lord, I love them despite everything. Please bless them ...

_____

_____

_____

Lord, thank you for teaching me ...

_____

_____

_____

Lord, I am sorry for my part in the situation ...

_____

_____

_____

Prayer of Requests

Day Three: _____/_____/_____

Lord, I need a miracle ...

_____

_____

_____

_____

_____

_____

_____

_____

_____

_____

_____

_____

_____

_____

_____

_____

Quiet Listening

Day Four: _____/_____/_____

Listen to God's quiet voice. What is he speaking to you?

_____

_____

_____

_____

_____

_____

_____

_____

_____

_____

What do you need to do to be obedient to his voice?

_____

_____

_____

Words of Promise

Day Five: _____/_____/_____

What has God promised you?

_____

_____

_____

_____

_____

_____

_____

_____

_____

_____

What does God want you to do to be a part of his promise?

_____

_____

_____

_____

Words of Power

Day Six: _____/_____/_____

God's promises are strong and sure. His Word tells me ...

_____

_____

_____

_____

_____

_____

_____

_____

_____

_____

_____

_____

_____

_____

Prayer of Thanksgiving

Day Seven: _____/_____/_____

List five things you are thankful for this week:

1. _____

2. _____

3. _____

4. _____

5. _____

What miracle, great or small, did God give you this week?

_____

_____

_____

_____

_____

Thank you, Lord, for all you have done for me this week ...

_____

_____

_____

_____

2 amazing
people who can
change your life

_____

_____

_____

_____

_____

_____

~ Ephesians 6:2-3

Hey friend ~

Want God's promise of long life and prosperity?

Then honor your parents *by living out the best parts of them*, by trying to emulate the essence of what they taught you.

I honor my father, who loved the Bible, by living by what God's word teaches. I honor my mother, who never let a day go by without finding some way to give to others or create something beautiful. Whatever differences I have had with my parents, I value the things they taught me: the Bible, loving others, giving, creating.

I honor my in-laws too, who taught me the meaning and importance of family. I also honor the sages of my church, who give me wisdom, encouragement, and love.

Reflection

What is God speaking to you about this week's verse?

_____

_____

_____

_____

_____

_____

_____

_____

_____

_____

What actions is God asking of you?

- ☐ _____
- ☐ _____
- ☐ _____
- ☐ _____
- ☐ _____

Prayer of Cleansing

Day One: _____/_____/_____

Lord, I love you ...

_____

_____

Lord, I am sorry for ...

_____

_____

_____

Lord, please forgive me. Help me to ...

_____

_____

Lord, thank you for ...

_____

_____

_____

_____

Prayer of Forgiveness

Day Two: _____ / _____ / _____

Lord, I forgive _____

Lord, I love them despite everything. Please bless them ...

_____

_____

_____

Lord, thank you for teaching me ...

_____

_____

_____

Lord, I am sorry for my part in the situation ...

_____

_____

_____

_____

Prayer of Requests
Day Three: ____/____/_____

Lord, I need a miracle ...

_____

_____

_____

_____

_____

_____

_____

_____

_____

_____

_____

_____

_____

_____

Quiet Listening

Day Four: _____ / _____ / _____

_____

_____

_____

_____

_____

_____

_____

_____

What do you need to do to be obedient to his voice?

_____

_____

_____

_____

Words of Promise

Day Five: _____/_____/_____

What has God promised you?

_____

_____

_____

_____

_____

_____

_____

_____

_____

_____

What does God want you to do to be a part of his promise?

_____

_____

_____

_____

Words of Power

Day Six: _____/_____/_____

God's promises are strong and sure. His Word tells me ...

_____

_____

_____

_____

_____

_____

_____

_____

_____

_____

_____

_____

_____

_____

_____

Prayer of Thanksgiving

Day Seven: _____ / _____ / _____

List five things you are thankful for this week:

1. _____

2. _____

3. _____

4. _____

5. _____

What miracle, great or small, did God give you this week?

_____

_____

_____

_____

_____

Thank you, Lord, for all you have done for me this week ...

_____

_____

_____

_____

Struggling to keep up with the Joneses? Here's the solution

_____

_____

_____

_____

_____

_____

~ Proverbs 11:4

A few words from Joy ...

Hey friend ~

I heard it said there are only three things you can do with money:

> *save it,*
>> *spend it,*
>>> *give it away.*

We certainly can't take it with us, nor can we use it to buy salvation.

The stress of striving for it, the struggle to keep up with everyone else, the endless grasping for more: let it all go.

Even here on earth, money is only a tool. It is God who solves our problems and provides our needs and deepest desires.

Reflection

What is God speaking to you about this week's verse?

_____

_____

_____

_____

_____

_____

_____

_____

_____

_____

_____

What actions is God asking of you?

☐ _____

☐ _____

☐ _____

☐ _____

☐ _____

Prayer of Cleansing

Day One: _____/_____/_____

Lord, I love you ...

_____

_____

Lord, I am sorry for ...

_____

_____

_____

Lord, please forgive me. Help me to ...

_____

Lord, thank you for ...

_____

_____

_____

Prayer of Forgiveness

Day Two: _____/_____/_____

| Lord, I forgive _____ |

| Lord, I love them despite everything. Please bless them ... |

_____

_____

_____

| Lord, thank you for teaching me ... |

_____

_____

_____

| Lord, I am sorry for my part in the situation ... |

_____

_____

_____

Prayer of Requests

Day Three: _____/_____/_____

Lord, I need a miracle ...

_____

_____

_____

_____

_____

_____

_____

_____

_____

_____

_____

_____

_____

_____

Quiet Listening

Day Four: _____ / _____ / _____

Listen to God's quiet voice. What is he speaking to you?

_____

_____

_____

_____

_____

_____

_____

_____

_____

What do you need to do to be obedient to his voice?

_____

_____

_____

Words of Promise

Day Five: _____/_____/_____

_____

_____

_____

_____

_____

_____

_____

_____

_____

What does God want you to do to be a part of his promise?

_____

_____

_____

_____

Words of Power

Day Six: _____ / _____ / _____

God's promises are strong and sure. His Word tells me ...

_____

_____

_____

_____

_____

_____

_____

_____

_____

_____

_____

_____

_____

_____

_____

_____

Prayer of Thanksgiving

Day Seven: _____/_____/_____

List five things you are thankful for this week:

1. _____

2. _____

3. _____

4. _____

5. _____

What miracle, great or small, did God give you this week?

_____

_____

_____

_____

_____

Thank you, Lord, for all you have done for me this week ...

_____

_____

_____

_____

Do get-rich-quick schemes ever work? Here's what God says about it

_____

_____

_____

_____

_____

_____

~ Psalms 37:7

A few words from Joy ...

Hey friend ~

I have learned this lesson over and over:

If I am desperate for what I want, I'm not ready to receive it.

If I finagle and cheat and connive to get my way, then thank God when he doesn't give it to me!

Wait on the Lord because his timing is perfect.

Reflection

_____
_____
_____
_____
_____
_____
_____
_____
_____
_____
_____
_____

What actions is God asking of you?

☐ _____
☐ _____
☐ _____
☐ _____
☐ _____

Prayer of Cleansing

Day One: _____/_____/_____

Lord, I love you ...

Lord, I am sorry for ...

Lord, please forgive me. Help me to ...

Lord, thank you for ...

Prayer of Forgiveness

Day Two: _____/_____/_____

Lord, I forgive _____

Lord, I love them despite everything. Please bless them ...

_____

_____

_____

Lord, thank you for teaching me ...

_____

_____

_____

Lord, I am sorry for my part in the situation ...

_____

_____

_____

_____

Prayer of Requests

Day Three: ____/____/_____

Lord, I need a miracle ...

_____

_____

_____

_____

_____

_____

_____

_____

_____

_____

_____

_____

_____

_____

Quiet Listening

Day Four: _____/_____/_____

Listen to God's quiet voice. What is he speaking to you?

_____

_____

_____

_____

_____

_____

_____

_____

_____

_____

What do you need to do to be obedient to his voice?

_____

_____

_____

_____

Words of Promise

Day Five: _____/_____/_____

What has God promised you?

_____

_____

_____

_____

_____

_____

_____

_____

_____

_____

What does God want you to do to be a part of his promise?

_____

_____

_____

_____

Words of Power

Day Six: _____/_____/_____

God's promises are strong and sure. His Word tells me ...

_____

_____

_____

_____

_____

_____

_____

_____

_____

_____

_____

_____

_____

_____

_____

Prayer of Thanksgiving

Day Seven: _____/_____/_____

List five things you are thankful for this week:

1. _____

2. _____

3. _____

4. _____

5. _____

What miracle, great or small, did God give you this week?

_____

_____

_____

_____

_____

Thank you, Lord, for all you have done for me this week ...

_____

_____

_____

_____

Week 16

Why thoughtful preparation can help you build your dream home

_____

_____

_____

_____

_____

_____

~ Proverbs 24:27

A few words from Joy ...

Hey friend ~

Phases to your financial life:

Building Stage: where you prepare your metaphorical fields

Prosperous Stage: where you enjoy the fruits of your labor

In my twenties, I meandered through life, not really knowing where I was going or what I wanted. By the time I knew I wanted to be a writer / publisher, I was in my thirties, married with three children. I had a full-time job and helped my husband with the homeschooling. Life was busy.

For me, I need to get my books written, build my audience, and lay the marketing groundwork before I can truly think about turning my home into the beautiful sanctuary I dream of.

Get these two things in the wrong order, and you will struggle financially. You won't have the financial groundwork to build a sustainable lifestyle.

Reflection

What is God speaking to you about this week's verse?

_____

_____

_____

_____

_____

_____

_____

_____

_____

_____

_____

_____

What actions is God asking of you?

☐ _____

☐ _____

☐ _____

☐ _____

☐ _____

Prayer of Cleansing

Day One: ____/____/_____

Lord, I love you ...

_____

_____

Lord, I am sorry for ...

_____

_____

_____

Lord, please forgive me. Help me to ...

_____

_____

Lord, thank you for ...

_____

_____

_____

_____

Prayer of Forgiveness

Day Two: _____/_____/_____

Lord, I forgive _____

Lord, I love them despite everything. Please bless them ...

_____

_____

_____

Lord, thank you for teaching me ...

_____

_____

_____

Lord, I am sorry for my part in the situation ...

_____

_____

_____

Prayer of Requests

Day Three: _____/_____/_____

Lord, I need a miracle ...

_____

_____

_____

_____

_____

_____

_____

_____

_____

_____

_____

_____

_____

_____

_____

Quiet Listening

Day Four: _____/_____/_____

Listen to God's quiet voice. What is he speaking to you?

_____

_____

_____

_____

_____

_____

_____

_____

What do you need to do to be obedient to his voice?

_____

_____

_____

Words of Promise

Day Five: _____/_____/_____

What has God promised you?

_____

_____

_____

_____

_____

_____

_____

_____

_____

_____

What does God want you to do to be a part of his promise?

_____

_____

_____

Words of Power

Day Six: _____/_____/_____

God's promises are strong and sure. His Word tells me ...

_____

_____

_____

_____

_____

_____

_____

_____

_____

_____

_____

_____

_____

_____

_____

Prayer of Thanksgiving

Day Seven: ____/____/_____

List five things you are thankful for this week:

1. _____

2. _____

3. _____

4. _____

5. _____

What miracle, great or small, did God give you this week?

_____

_____

_____

_____

_____

Thank you, Lord, for all you have done for me this week ...

_____

_____

_____

_____

Why trusting
God's plans will
get you where
you need to be

_____

_____

_____

_____

_____

_____

~ Jeremiah 29:11

A few words from Joy ...

Hey friend ~

My confession: I have a tendency to rely only on myself.

I see myself marching alone, trying to be successful. Deep down, I don't believe anyone else will help me, that anyone cares.

But God has a plan to make me prosper. If only I would turn to him.

He has a plan for you too. Ask him, and he will show you the path you need to take to make it happen. Sometimes it is only the first step, but if you obey, he will show you the next step after that.

Reflection

What is God speaking to you about this week's verse?

_____

_____

_____

_____

_____

_____

_____

_____

_____

_____

What actions is God asking of you?

☐ _____

☐ _____

☐ _____

☐ _____

☐ _____

Prayer of Cleansing

Day One: _____/_____/_____

Lord, I love you ...

_____

_____

Lord, I am sorry for ...

_____

_____

_____

Lord, please forgive me. Help me to ...

_____

Lord, thank you for ...

_____

_____

_____

Prayer of Forgiveness

Day Two: _____/_____/_____

Lord, I forgive _____

Lord, I love them despite everything. Please bless them ...

_____

_____

_____

Lord, thank you for teaching me ...

_____

_____

_____

Lord, I am sorry for my part in the situation ...

_____

_____

_____

Prayer of Requests

Day Three: _____/_____/_____

> Lord, I need a miracle ...

_____

_____

_____

_____

_____

_____

_____

_____

_____

_____

_____

_____

_____

Quiet Listening

Day Four: _____/_____/_____

Listen to God's quiet voice. What is he speaking to you?

_____

_____

_____

_____

_____

_____

_____

_____

_____

What do you need to do to be obedient to his voice?

_____

_____

_____

_____

Words of Promise

Day Five: _____ / _____ / _____

What has God promised you?

_____

_____

_____

_____

_____

_____

_____

_____

_____

What does God want you to do to be a part of his promise?

_____

_____

_____

_____

Words of Power

Day Six: _____/_____/_____

God's promises are strong and sure. His Word tells me ...

_____

_____

_____

_____

_____

_____

_____

_____

_____

_____

_____

_____

_____

_____

Prayer of Thanksgiving

Day Seven: _____/_____/_____

List five things you are thankful for this week:

1. _____

2. _____

3. _____

4. _____

5. _____

What miracle, great or small, did God give you this week?

_____

_____

_____

_____

_____

Thank you, Lord, for all you have done for me this week ...

_____

_____

_____

_____

Week 18

Why your financial plans may be crippling your future

~ Proverbs 27:1

Hey friend ~

I work at a tech firm that makes software for hospitals and doctor's offices. The big word that every team tries to become is agile. Gurus study agile methodologies. Teams take classes. People argue: we can't do that; it isn't agile.

Plans can change – the business needs to respond to the growing market and the development team needs to be ready to change with it.

Sometimes, as Christians, we need to be ready for whatever God has planned. He has his finger on the market, he knows the best play, and we need to be ready to move when he calls.

Hmm, easier said than done?

Reflection

What is God speaking to you about this week's verse?

_____

_____

_____

_____

_____

_____

_____

_____

_____

_____

What actions is God asking of you?

☐ _____

☐ _____

☐ _____

☐ _____

☐ _____

Prayer of Cleansing

Day One: _____/_____/_____

Lord, I love you ...

_____

_____

Lord, I am sorry for ...

_____

_____

_____

Lord, please forgive me. Help me to ...

_____

_____

Lord, thank you for ...

_____

_____

_____

Prayer of Forgiveness

Day Two: _____/_____/_____

> Lord, I forgive _____

> Lord, I love them despite everything. Please bless them ...

_____

_____

_____

_____

> Lord, thank you for teaching me ...

_____

_____

_____

_____

> Lord, I am sorry for my part in the situation ...

_____

_____

_____

_____

Prayer of Requests
Day Three: ___/___/_____

Lord, I need a miracle ...

_____

_____

_____

_____

_____

_____

_____

_____

_____

_____

_____

_____

_____

_____

Quiet Listening

Day Four: _____/_____/_____

_____

_____

_____

_____

_____

_____

_____

_____

_____

What do you need to do to be obedient to his voice?

_____

_____

_____

_____

Words of Promise

Day Five: _____/_____/_____

What has God promised you?

_____

_____

_____

_____

_____

_____

_____

_____

_____

_____

What does God want you to do to be a part of his promise?

_____

_____

_____

_____

Words of Power

Day Six: _____/_____/_____

God's promises are strong and sure. His Word tells me ...

_____

_____

_____

_____

_____

_____

_____

_____

_____

_____

_____

_____

_____

Prayer of Thanksgiving

Day Seven: _____/_____/_____

List five things you are thankful for this week:

1. _____

2. _____

3. _____

4. _____

5. _____

What miracle, great or small, did God give you this week?

_____

_____

_____

_____

_____

_____

Thank you, Lord, for all you have done for me this week ...

_____

_____

_____

_____

Week 19

The ultimate
guide to
mastering your
financial plans

_____

_____

_____

_____

_____

_____

~ Proverbs 19:21

A few words from Joy ...

Hey friend ~

I'm notorious for reading a business book or a marketing strategy and jumping on the new bandwagon. I make a quick plan, using what I learned, and forget to (1) check in with God and (2) check in with my husband, who is also my business partner.

Then my half-baked plans fail.

When am I going to learn to slow down and think things through?

Planning is good! Budgets, debt payoff schedules, business plans, schooling and career plans, or maybe just a quick task list for your day.

However, when you plan, *invite God to be part of it*. Ask him to reveal his plan for you. Listen.

Reflection

What is God speaking to you about this week's verse?

_____

_____

_____

_____

_____

_____

_____

_____

_____

_____

What actions is God asking of you?

☐ _____

☐ _____

☐ _____

☐ _____

☐ _____

Prayer of Cleansing

Day One: _____ / _____ / _____

Lord, I love you ...

_____

_____

_____

Lord, I am sorry for ...

_____

_____

_____

_____

Lord, please forgive me. Help me to ...

_____

_____

Lord, thank you for ...

_____

_____

_____

_____

Prayer of Forgiveness

Day Two: _____/_____/_____

Lord, I forgive _____

Lord, I love them despite everything. Please bless them ...

_____

_____

_____

Lord, thank you for teaching me ...

_____

_____

_____

Lord, I am sorry for my part in the situation ...

_____

_____

_____

Prayer of Requests

Day Three: _____/_____/_____

Lord, I need a miracle ...

_____

_____

_____

_____

_____

_____

_____

_____

_____

_____

_____

_____

_____

_____

Quiet Listening

Day Four: _____/_____/_____

Listen to God's quiet voice. What is he speaking to you?

_____

_____

_____

_____

_____

_____

_____

_____

_____

_____

What do you need to do to be obedient to his voice?

_____

_____

_____

_____

Words of Promise

Day Five: _____/_____/_____

What has God promised you?

_____

_____

_____

_____

_____

_____

_____

_____

_____

What does God want you to do to be a part of his promise?

_____

_____

_____

_____

Words of Power

Day Six: _____ / _____ / _____

God's promises are strong and sure. His Word tells me ...

_____

_____

_____

_____

_____

_____

_____

_____

_____

_____

_____

_____

_____

_____

Prayer of Thanksgiving

Day Seven: _____/_____/_____

List five things you are thankful for this week:

1. _____

2. _____

3. _____

4. _____

5. _____

What miracle, great or small, did God give you this week?

_____

_____

_____

_____

_____

Thank you, Lord, for all you have done for me this week ...

_____

_____

_____

_____

Week 20

How to plan for prosperity — God's life-changing way

_____

_____

_____

_____

_____

_____

~ Proverbs 21:5

Hey friend ~

There's no one-size-fits-all solution. No get-rich-quick scheme.

It's about doing the small things, the hard things, and making careful plans, thinking things through. Praying about the plan and the steps involved. Seeking God's input.

Like losing weight for good, you can only gain lasting financial freedom with these four things:

- Careful planning
- Good daily habits
- Perseverance
- Time

Once you've made the plan, let it sit for week, maybe a month, and then review it again before implementing it.

Reflection

What is God speaking to you about this week's verse?

_____

_____

_____

_____

_____

_____

_____

_____

_____

_____

_____

What actions is God asking of you?

☐ _____

☐ _____

☐ _____

☐ _____

☐ _____

Prayer of Cleansing

Day One: ____/____/_____

Lord, I love you ...

_____

_____

_____

Lord, I am sorry for ...

_____

_____

_____

Lord, please forgive me. Help me to ...

_____

Lord, thank you for ...

_____

_____

_____

Prayer of Forgiveness

Day Two: _____/_____/_____

| Lord, I forgive _____ |

| Lord, I love them despite everything. Please bless them ... |

_____

_____

_____

| Lord, thank you for teaching me ... |

_____

_____

_____

| Lord, I am sorry for my part in the situation ... |

_____

_____

_____

Prayer of Requests

Day Three: _____ / _____ / _____

Lord, I need a miracle ...

Quiet Listening

Day Four: _____/_____/_____

> Listen to God's quiet voice. What is he speaking to you?

_____

_____

_____

_____

_____

_____

_____

_____

_____

_____

> What do you need to do to be obedient to his voice?

_____

_____

_____

_____

Words of Promise

Day Five: _____/_____/_____

What has God promised you?

_____

_____

_____

_____

_____

_____

_____

_____

_____

_____

What does God want you to do to be a part of his promise?

_____

_____

_____

_____

Words of Power

Day Six: _____/_____/_____

God's promises are strong and sure. His Word tells me ...

_____

_____

_____

_____

_____

_____

_____

_____

_____

_____

_____

_____

_____

_____

_____

_____

Prayer of Thanksgiving

Day Seven: _____/_____/_____

List five things you are thankful for this week:

1. _____

2. _____

3. _____

4. _____

5. _____

What miracle, great or small, did God give you this week?

_____

_____

_____

_____

_____

Thank you, Lord, for all you have done for me this week ...

_____

_____

_____

_____

Week 21

The #1 daring strategy to getting rich without losing your soul

~ Proverbs 11:24-25

A few words from Joy ...

Hey friend ~

Worrying about money?

Whenever you find yourself getting desperate, feeling frustrated, fretting over how little you have, it's a good time to find someone with more financial problems than you and help them out.

This action is the one thing to cut through the spiritual turmoil related to money that builds in us. Greed. Desperation. Worry.

Giving reminds of things more powerful: gratitude, kindness, love, God's immense provision.

Reflection

What is God speaking to you about this week's verse?

_____

_____

_____

_____

_____

_____

_____

_____

_____

_____

_____

What actions is God asking of you?

☐ _____

☐ _____

☐ _____

☐ _____

☐ _____

Prayer of Cleansing

Day One: _____/_____/_____

> Lord, I love you ...

_____

_____

> Lord, I am sorry for ...

_____

_____

_____

> Lord, please forgive me. Help me to ...

_____

_____

> Lord, thank you for ...

_____

_____

_____

Prayer of Forgiveness

Day Two: _____ / _____ / _____

Lord, I forgive _____

Lord, I love them despite everything. Please bless them ...

_____

_____

_____

Lord, thank you for teaching me ...

_____

_____

_____

Lord, I am sorry for my part in the situation ...

_____

_____

_____

Prayer of Requests
Day Three: ____/____/_____

Lord, I need a miracle ...

_____

_____

_____

_____

_____

_____

_____

_____

_____

_____

_____

_____

_____

_____

_____

_____

_____

Quiet Listening

Day Four: _____/_____/_____

_____

_____

_____

_____

_____

_____

_____

_____

_____

What do you need to do to be obedient to his voice?

_____

_____

_____

_____

Words of Promise

Day Five: _____ / _____ / _____

What has God promised you?

_____

_____

_____

_____

_____

_____

_____

_____

_____

_____

What does God want you to do to be a part of his promise?

_____

_____

_____

Words of Power

Day Six: _____ / _____ / _____

God's promises are strong and sure. His Word tells me ...

_____

_____

_____

_____

_____

_____

_____

_____

_____

_____

_____

_____

_____

_____

Prayer of Thanksgiving

Day Seven: _____/_____/_____

List five things you are thankful for this week:

1. _____

2. _____

3. _____

4. _____

5. _____

What miracle, great or small, did God give you this week?

_____

_____

_____

_____

_____

Thank you, Lord, for all you have done for me this week ...

_____

_____

_____

Week 22

Solomon's brazen guide to investing in today's world

~ Proverbs 19:17

A few words from Joy ...

Hey friend ~

In this day and age, it's a brazen investment strategy: lending to the One who holds the world in his hands.

It's not just about giving our money to the poor. It is about *investing in people*. Caring about what the Lord cares about.

Watch people's faces and body language. When you see discouragement, pain, heartache, find some way to turn it around for them. Be purposeful with your actions.

He promises to repay you.

Reflection

What is God speaking to you about this week's verse?

_____

_____

_____

_____

_____

_____

_____

_____

_____

_____

_____

What actions is God asking of you?

- ☐ _____
- ☐ _____
- ☐ _____
- ☐ _____
- ☐ _____

Prayer of Cleansing

Day One: _____ / _____ / _____

Lord, I love you ...

_____

_____

_____

Lord, I am sorry for ...

_____

_____

_____

Lord, please forgive me. Help me to ...

_____

_____

Lord, thank you for ...

_____

_____

_____

Prayer of Forgiveness

Day Two: _____/_____/_____

Lord, I forgive _____

Lord, I love them despite everything. Please bless them ...

_____

_____

_____

Lord, thank you for teaching me ...

_____

_____

_____

Lord, I am sorry for my part in the situation ...

_____

_____

_____

Prayer of Requests

Day Three: _____/_____/_____

Lord, I need a miracle ...

Quiet Listening

Day Four: _____/_____/_____

Listen to God's quiet voice. What is he speaking to you?

_____

_____

_____

_____

_____

_____

_____

_____

_____

What do you need to do to be obedient to his voice?

_____

_____

_____

_____

Words of Promise

Day Five: _____ / _____ / _____

What has God promised you?

_____

_____

_____

_____

_____

_____

_____

_____

_____

_____

What does God want you to do to be a part of his promise?

_____

_____

_____

_____

Words of Power

Day Six: _____ / _____ / _____

God's promises are strong and sure. His Word tells me ...

_____

_____

_____

_____

_____

_____

_____

_____

_____

_____

_____

_____

_____

_____

_____

Prayer of Thanksgiving

Day Seven: _____/_____/_____

List five things you are thankful for this week:

1. _____

2. _____

3. _____

4. _____

5. _____

What miracle, great or small, did God give you this week?

_____

_____

_____

_____

_____

Thank you, Lord, for all you have done for me this week ...

_____

_____

_____

_____

Week 23

2 things only
the prosperous
understand
about finding
enduring riches

_____

_____

_____

_____

_____

_____

~ Proverbs 11:28, 30a

Hey friend ~

A righteous man is a tree by a river, his roots reaching down deep into the earth, his leaves a beautiful, vibrant green. When the drought comes and the river dries up, he still thrives.

You're probably asking:

what does this have to do with money mindset, Joy?

To be prosperous, to truly thrive, to find enduring riches, we must do two things:

1. Don't trust in your money
2. Live righteously

We can't trust money to supply our needs, and the more we do trust it, the more it will wither and fade, slipping between our fingers. Only the everlasting water Jesus offers can make us thrive. He is the deep spring from which we can always drink.

Reflection

What is God speaking to you about this week's verse?

_____

_____

_____

_____

_____

_____

_____

_____

_____

_____

What actions is God asking of you?

- ☐ _____
- ☐ _____
- ☐ _____
- ☐ _____
- ☐ _____

Prayer of Cleansing

Day One: _____/_____/_____

> Lord, I love you ...

> Lord, I am sorry for ...

> Lord, please forgive me. Help me to ...

> Lord, thank you for ...

Prayer of Forgiveness

Day Two: ____/____/_____

Lord, I forgive _____

Lord, I love them despite everything. Please bless them ...

_____

_____

_____

Lord, thank you for teaching me ...

_____

_____

_____

Lord, I am sorry for my part in the situation ...

_____

_____

_____

Prayer of Requests

Day Three: ____/____/_____

Lord, I need a miracle ...

_____

_____

_____

_____

_____

_____

_____

_____

_____

_____

_____

_____

_____

_____

_____

Quiet Listening

Day Four: _____/_____/_____

Listen to God's quiet voice. What is he speaking to you?

_____

_____

_____

_____

_____

_____

_____

_____

What do you need to do to be obedient to his voice?

_____

_____

_____

_____

Words of Promise

Day Five: _____/_____/_____

What has God promised you?

_____

_____

_____

_____

_____

_____

_____

_____

_____

_____

What does God want you to do to be a part of his promise?

_____

_____

_____

_____

Words of Power

Day Six: _____/_____/_____

God's promises are strong and sure. His Word tells me ...

_____

_____

_____

_____

_____

_____

_____

_____

_____

_____

_____

_____

_____

_____

Prayer of Thanksgiving

Day Seven: _____/_____/_____

List five things you are thankful for this week:

1. _____

2. _____

3. _____

4. _____

5. _____

What miracle, great or small, did God give you this week?

_____

_____

_____

_____

_____

Thank you, Lord, for all you have done for me this week ...

_____

_____

_____

Week 24

How to pray like a warrior and find God's enduring answers to your problems

~ Matthew 7:7-8

Hey friend ~

I haven't found anywhere where God said it wasn't in his power or in his will to answer prayer. Except when there was disobedience or lack of faith. From providing food to opening the womb, from healing the sick to raising the dead, God always said yes ...

... eventually.

Sometimes there were years and years of waiting and living by faith.

But eventually, Abraham and Sarah had a son. Joseph's prophetic dreams came true – after he was sold into slavery and then thrown into jail. The children of Israel made it to the Promised Land.

Eventually, a virgin conceived and God Incarnate came down and died for our sins.

Why does God make us wait? Sometimes to perfect our faith. Sometimes to show that nothing else, no one else, could have provided the miracle.

It is always the hand of our all-powerful, all-knowing God who makes the miracles happen.

Reflection

What is God speaking to you about this week's verse?

_____

_____

_____

_____

_____

_____

_____

_____

_____

_____

What actions is God asking of you?

☐ _____

☐ _____

☐ _____

☐ _____

☐ _____

Prayer of Cleansing

Day One: _____ / _____ / _____

Lord, I love you ...

_____

_____

Lord, I am sorry for ...

_____

_____

_____

Lord, please forgive me. Help me to ...

_____

Lord, thank you for ...

_____

_____

_____

Prayer of Forgiveness

Day Two: _____/_____/_____

Lord, I forgive _____

Lord, I love them despite everything. Please bless them ...

_____

_____

_____

Lord, thank you for teaching me ...

_____

_____

_____

Lord, I am sorry for my part in the situation ...

_____

_____

_____

Prayer of Requests

Day Three: _____/_____/_____

Lord, I need a miracle ...

_____

_____

_____

_____

_____

_____

_____

_____

_____

_____

_____

_____

_____

_____

_____

Quiet Listening

Day Four: _____/_____/_____

Listen to God's quiet voice. What is he speaking to you?

_____

_____

_____

_____

_____

_____

_____

_____

What do you need to do to be obedient to his voice?

_____

_____

_____

Words of Promise

Day Five: _____/_____/_____

What has God promised you?

_____

_____

_____

_____

_____

_____

_____

_____

_____

What does God want you to do to be a part of his promise?

_____

_____

_____

_____

Words of Power

Day Six: _____/_____/_____

God's promises are strong and sure. His Word tells me ...

_____

_____

_____

_____

_____

_____

_____

_____

_____

_____

_____

_____

_____

_____

Prayer of Thanksgiving

Day Seven: _____/_____/_____

List five things you are thankful for this week:

1. _____

2. _____

3. _____

4. _____

5. _____

What miracle, great or small, did God give you this week?

_____

_____

_____

_____

_____

Thank you, Lord, for all you have done for me this week ...

_____

_____

_____

_____

Crying to God for help? Here's God's incredible promise to you

_____

_____

_____

_____

_____

_____

_____

~ Psalm 145:19

A few words from Joy ...

Hey friend ~

When you love God with all your heart, all your soul, all your mind, your deepest desires are in tune with his plans and desires. He places dreams and desires in your heart, and he wants to fulfill them through you.

But what does it really mean to fear God?

It's closely related to awe. When you see how big God is, how tremendously awesome, how beautiful and powerful, how majestic, you begin to see how small you are. You begin to tremble in his presence.

This is when you are spiritually in a place for God to fulfill his promises to you.

Reflection

What is God speaking to you about this week's verse?

_____

_____

_____

_____

_____

_____

_____

_____

_____

_____

What actions is God asking of you?

☐ _____

☐ _____

☐ _____

☐ _____

☐ _____

Prayer of Cleansing
Day One: ____/____/_____

Lord, I love you ...

_____

_____

_____

Lord, I am sorry for ...

_____

_____

_____

Lord, please forgive me. Help me to ...

_____

_____

Lord, thank you for ...

_____

_____

_____

Prayer of Forgiveness

Day Two: ____/____/_____

Lord, I forgive _____

Lord, I love them despite everything. Please bless them ...

_____

_____

_____

_____

Lord, thank you for teaching me ...

_____

_____

_____

_____

Lord, I am sorry for my part in the situation ...

_____

_____

_____

_____

Prayer of Requests

Day Three: _____/_____/_____

Lord, I need a miracle ...

Quiet Listening
Day Four: _____/_____/_____

> Listen to God's quiet voice. What is he speaking to you?

_____

_____

_____

_____

_____

_____

_____

_____

_____

> What do you need to do to be obedient to his voice?

_____

_____

_____

_____

Words of Promise

Day Five: _____ / _____ / _____

What has God promised you?

_____

_____

_____

_____

_____

_____

_____

_____

What does God want you to do to be a part of his promise?

_____

_____

_____

Words of Power

Day Six: _____ / _____ / _____

> God's promises are strong and sure. His Word tells me ...

_____

_____

_____

_____

_____

_____

_____

_____

_____

_____

_____

_____

_____

_____

Prayer of Thanksgiving

Day Seven: _____/_____/_____

List five things you are thankful for this week:

1. _____

2. _____

3. _____

4. _____

5. _____

What miracle, great or small, did God give you this week?

_____

_____

_____

_____

_____

Thank you, Lord, for all you have done for me this week ...

_____

_____

_____

_____

Week 26

1 daring promise to remember when life gets tough

~ Malachi 3:10

A few words from Joy ...

Hey friend ~

Why are we covering this again?

Well, that was in Proverbs. This is Malachi.

Since the Bible says it more than once, I figured we need to be reminded. Paying tithe is a lesson I've had to learn many times over. When the bills come rolling in, I have gotten weak and backed away.

It's easy to slip away from tithing when God didn't seem to fulfill his promises right away, when money got tighter. However, you need to press in and stick to your plan.

Cling to God's promise and don't give up.

Reflection

What is God speaking to you about this week's verse?

_____

_____

_____

_____

_____

_____

_____

_____

_____

_____

_____

What actions is God asking of you?

☐ _____

☐ _____

☐ _____

☐ _____

☐ _____

Prayer of Cleansing

Day One: _____ / _____ / _____

Lord, I love you ...

_____

_____

_____

Lord, I am sorry for ...

_____

_____

_____

Lord, please forgive me. Help me to ...

_____

_____

Lord, thank you for ...

_____

_____

_____

Prayer of Forgiveness

Day Two: ____/____/_____

Lord, I forgive _____

Lord, I love them despite everything. Please bless them ...

_____

_____

_____

Lord, thank you for teaching me ...

_____

_____

_____

Lord, I am sorry for my part in the situation ...

_____

_____

_____

Prayer of Requests
Day Three: ____/____/_____

Lord, I need a miracle ...

_____

_____

_____

_____

_____

_____

_____

_____

_____

_____

_____

_____

_____

_____

Quiet Listening

Day Four: _____/_____/_____

> Listen to God's quiet voice. What is he speaking to you?

_____

_____

_____

_____

_____

_____

_____

_____

_____

> What do you need to do to be obedient to his voice?

_____

_____

_____

_____

Words of Promise

Day Five: _____/_____/_____

What has God promised you?

_____

_____

_____

_____

_____

_____

_____

_____

_____

What does God want you to do to be a part of his promise?

_____

_____

_____

_____

Words of Power

Day Six: _____ / _____ / _____

God's promises are strong and sure. His Word tells me ...

_____

_____

_____

_____

_____

_____

_____

_____

_____

_____

_____

_____

_____

Day Seven: ____/____/_____

| List five things you are thankful for this week: |

1. _____

2. _____

3. _____

4. _____

5. _____

| What miracle, great or small, did God give you this week? |

| Thank you, Lord, for all you have done for me this week ... |

Week 27

Do you have enough faith to move mountains? Here's what your Heavenly Father says about it

~ Luke 17:6

Hey friend ~

Honestly, I feel more like the man in the Bible who cried out to Jesus, "Lord, I believe. Please help my unbelief (Mark 9:24)."

Most of the time, I struggle to believe God would do miracles *for me*. I feel like I'm asking too much just to have enough money to cover my expenses and put something into savings.

I feel more like Gideon who had so little trust in his ability to hear God's voice that he questioned everything. I feel like Moses who protested he couldn't speak well enough to carry God's message. I feel like Peter who stepped out of the boat only to end up nearly drowning. Yet God still used each and every one of them.

All they needed – and all you need – is a small kernel of faith the size of a mustard seed.

It's okay to cry out to Jesus and say, "Lord, I believe. Please help my unbelief."

That's enough for him to work with.

Reflection

What is God speaking to you about this week's verse?

_____

_____

_____

_____

_____

_____

_____

_____

_____

_____

_____

What actions is God asking of you?

☐ _____

☐ _____

☐ _____

☐ _____

☐ _____

Prayer of Cleansing

Day One: ____/____/_____

> Lord, I love you ...

> Lord, I am sorry for ...

> Lord, please forgive me. Help me to ...

> Lord, thank you for ...

Prayer of Forgiveness

Day Two: _____/_____/_____

Lord, I forgive _____

Lord, I love them despite everything. Please bless them ...

_____

_____

_____

Lord, thank you for teaching me ...

_____

_____

_____

Lord, I am sorry for my part in the situation ...

_____

_____

_____

Prayer of Requests
Day Three: ____/____/_____

Lord, I need a miracle ...

_____

_____

_____

_____

_____

_____

_____

_____

_____

_____

_____

_____

_____

_____

Quiet Listening

Day Four: _____/_____/_____

Listen to God's quiet voice. What is he speaking to you?

_____

_____

_____

_____

_____

_____

_____

_____

What do you need to do to be obedient to his voice?

_____

_____

_____

_____

Words of Promise

Day Five: _____/_____/_____

What has God promised you?

_____

_____

_____

_____

_____

_____

_____

_____

_____

_____

What does God want you to do to be a part of his promise?

_____

_____

_____

Words of Power

Day Six: _____/_____/_____

God's promises are strong and sure. His Word tells me ...

_____

_____

_____

_____

_____

_____

_____

_____

_____

_____

_____

_____

_____

_____

Prayer of Thanksgiving

Day Seven: _____/_____/_____

List five things you are thankful for this week:

1. _____

2. _____

3. _____

4. _____

5. _____

What miracle, great or small, did God give you this week?

_____

_____

_____

_____

_____

Thank you, Lord, for all you have done for me this week ...

_____

_____

_____

_____

The ultimate
guide to
answered prayer

~ John 15:7

A few words from Joy ...

Hey friend ~

Throughout the Bible, God promises to fulfill our deepest desires, but it always comes with an if-statement:

> if we put him first,
> > if we abide in him,
> > > if we delight in him,
> > > > if we reverence and trust him ...

Just like how I often tell my kids, "Yes, you can go outside to play if you give me a great big hug first. Yes, you can have a bowl of ice cream or watch a movie, but first, give me a kiss."

The key to answered prayer is abiding in him.

Reflection

What is God speaking to you about this week's verse?

_____

_____

_____

_____

_____

_____

_____

_____

_____

_____

What actions is God asking of you?

☐ _____

☐ _____

☐ _____

☐ _____

☐ _____

Prayer of Cleansing

Day One: _____/_____/_____

Lord, I love you ...

_____

_____

Lord, I am sorry for ...

_____

_____

_____

Lord, please forgive me. Help me to ...

_____

Lord, thank you for ...

_____

_____

_____

Prayer of Forgiveness

Day Two: _____/_____/_____

Lord, I forgive _____

Lord, I love them despite everything. Please bless them ...

_____

_____

_____

Lord, thank you for teaching me ...

_____

_____

_____

Lord, I am sorry for my part in the situation ...

_____

_____

_____

Prayer of Requests

Day Three: _____/_____/_____

Lord, I need a miracle ...

_____

_____

_____

_____

_____

_____

_____

_____

_____

_____

_____

_____

_____

_____

Quiet Listening

Day Four: _____/_____/_____

_____

_____

_____

_____

_____

_____

_____

_____

_____

_____

_____

_____

Words of Promise

Day Five: _____/_____/_____

What has God promised you?

_____

_____

_____

_____

_____

_____

_____

_____

_____

_____

What does God want you to do to be a part of his promise?

_____

_____

_____

Words of Power

God's promises are strong and sure. His Word tells me ...

_____

_____

_____

_____

_____

_____

_____

_____

_____

_____

_____

_____

_____

_____

Prayer of Thanksgiving

Day Seven: _____/_____/_____

List five things you are thankful for this week:

1. _____
2. _____
3. _____
4. _____
5. _____

What miracle, great or small, did God give you this week?

_____

_____

_____

_____

_____

Thank you, Lord, for all you have done for me this week ...

_____

_____

_____

_____

Week 29

How to be a
fearless prayer
warrior after
God's own
heart

_____

_____

_____

_____

_____

_____

_____

~ Psalm 37:4

Hey friend ~

In church one day, a word of knowledge was spoken out loud, saying that someone would be given visions, that someone would see God's face.

I somehow knew this was me, and my internal response was fear and rejection. I did not want to see God's face.

And I immediately regretted my reaction. "Lord, if you want to show me your face, then I want to see you."

Nothing happened, and I thought God changed his mind.

Church was ending, and when I stood, I happened to see a baby – no more than six months old – climbing on his grandfather's lap. The grandfather had a snowy white beard, and the baby was mesmerized and delighted by this beard. He kept reaching for it, wrapping his fingers in it, clinging to it.

The wonder on his little face was awesome to behold. At that moment, I saw myself on God's lap, reaching for his face.

Delight is not a strong enough word for what I felt. Can you delight in God that way?

Reflection

_____

_____

_____

_____

_____

_____

_____

_____

_____

_____

What actions is God asking of you?

- ☐ _____
- ☐ _____
- ☐ _____
- ☐ _____
- ☐ _____

Prayer of Cleansing

Day One: _____/_____/_____

Lord, I love you ...

_____

_____

Lord, I am sorry for ...

_____

_____

_____

Lord, please forgive me. Help me to ...

_____

Lord, thank you for ...

_____

_____

_____

Prayer of Forgiveness

Day Two: _____ / _____ / _____

Lord, I forgive _____

Lord, I love them despite everything. Please bless them ...

_____

_____

_____

Lord, thank you for teaching me ...

_____

_____

_____

Lord, I am sorry for my part in the situation ...

_____

_____

_____

Prayer of Requests

Day Three: _____/_____/_____

> Lord, I need a miracle ...

_____

_____

_____

_____

_____

_____

_____

_____

_____

_____

_____

_____

_____

Quiet Listening

Day Four: _____/_____/_____

Listen to God's quiet voice. What is he speaking to you?

_____

_____

_____

_____

_____

_____

_____

_____

_____

_____

What do you need to do to be obedient to his voice?

_____

_____

_____

_____

Words of Promise

Day Five: _____/_____/_____

What has God promised you?

_____

_____

_____

_____

_____

_____

_____

_____

_____

_____

What does God want you to do to be a part of his promise?

_____

_____

_____

_____

Words of Power

Day Six: _____/_____/_____

God's promises are strong and sure. His Word tells me ...

_____

_____

_____

_____

_____

_____

_____

_____

_____

_____

_____

_____

_____

_____

Prayer of Thanksgiving

Day Seven: _____/_____/_____

List five things you are thankful for this week:

1. _____

2. _____

3. _____

4. _____

5. _____

What miracle, great or small, did God give you this week?

_____

_____

_____

_____

_____

Thank you, Lord, for all you have done for me this week ...

_____

_____

_____

_____

Week 30

How to prioritize like a boss and why money will never really matter

_____

_____

_____

_____

_____

_____

_____

~ Matthew 6:31-33

Hey friend ~

God created you with the purpose to love him, but he designed you with the capacity to create. Made in his image, you have both *the propensity and the need to create*: music, art, stories, laughter, games.

But you were not designed to *achieve*.

Achievements may come along the way – a pat on the back, a good grade in school, a promotion, an award for your art or book or music – but these are not what your soul needs.

It is the act of creation that fuels you.

So when God asks us to seek first the Kingdom of God, we need to let go of the worldly focus on achievements. Become a child again, when you would play with no thought for yourself, just the joy of painting or drawing or building with blocks or telling stories or making a mess.

In God's Kingdom, we create something beautiful, and the only thing we want is the Father's approval. We want his smile on us, like a father to his child.

Seek this first, and everything else will be given to you.

Reflection

_____

_____

_____

_____

_____

_____

_____

_____

_____

_____

What actions is God asking of you?

☐ _____

☐ _____

☐ _____

☐ _____

☐ _____

Prayer of Cleansing

Day One: _____ / _____ / _____

| Lord, I love you ... |

_____

_____

| Lord, I am sorry for ... |

_____

_____

_____

| Lord, please forgive me. Help me to ... |

_____

_____

| Lord, thank you for ... |

_____

_____

_____

Prayer of Forgiveness

Day Two: _____/_____/_____

Lord, I forgive _____

Lord, I love them despite everything. Please bless them ...

_____

_____

_____

Lord, thank you for teaching me ...

_____

_____

_____

Lord, I am sorry for my part in the situation ...

_____

_____

_____

Prayer of Requests

Day Three: _____/_____/_____

Lord, I need a miracle ...

_____

_____

_____

_____

_____

_____

_____

_____

_____

_____

_____

_____

_____

Quiet Listening

Day Four: _____/_____/_____

Listen to God's quiet voice. What is he speaking to you?

_____

_____

_____

_____

_____

_____

_____

_____

What do you need to do to be obedient to his voice?

_____

_____

_____

Words of Promise

Day Five: _____/_____/_____

What has God promised you?

_____

_____

_____

_____

_____

_____

_____

_____

_____

_____

What does God want you to do to be a part of his promise?

_____

_____

_____

_____

Words of Power

God's promises are strong and sure. His Word tells me ...

_____

_____

_____

_____

_____

_____

_____

_____

_____

_____

_____

_____

_____

_____

_____

_____

Prayer of Thanksgiving

Day Seven: _____/_____/_____

List five things you are thankful for this week:

1. _____

2. _____

3. _____

4. _____

5. _____

What miracle, great or small, did God give you this week?

_____

_____

_____

_____

Thank you, Lord, for all you have done for me this week ...

_____

_____

_____

Dear friend ~

Thank you so much for taking a chance on this prayer journal and for working through it to the end. I hope you got as much out of this as I did.

I want to encourage you to work through this book again. Money matters never go away, and as you've worked through these scriptures and dealt with each subject, you have likely learned much.

Going back to the first topics, like budgeting and managing debt, will give you a deeper understanding of money. You can apply the lessons to your situation even better than you did the first time.

Just grab a 300+ page notebook, and use this book as a guide.

Hugs,
Joy

About J.J. Thomas

Joy loves spending time with her family, singing, painting, dancing, and telling silly stories. She makes up songs about turtles for her children and wishes she knew how to play the piano. Someday, she wants to make the world a better place.

Dream
Catcher

Simple Prayers to Open Doors,
Break Shackles, Create Miracles

J.J. Thomas

Remember when you still believed in your dreams?

You were going to be a teacher, a veterinarian, an astronaut, the first female president, the best mommy ever. You wanted to be someone's hero and make the world a better place.

Now life is nothing but a rat race, your job is unfulfilling, and you barely have time to kiss the kids when you tuck them in at night, let alone be their hero. What happened to your dreams?

God hasn't forgotten you. He has awesome plans to prosper you, plans full of hope for your future (Jeremiah 29:11).

Learn the secrets to catching your dreams:

* Why praying without power doesn't work – and the one thing you can change today to get a direct line to God's throne room

* The Key to unlocking your full potential and opening the door to the path God has in store for you – and it's not what you think

* The Jericho Battle Plan that will change the way you live every day of your life

* The Prophetic Voice that opens doors, creates miracles, and allows your wildest dreams to come true

Get your copy from your favorite bookseller and start making your dreams come true.

Made in the USA
Columbia, SC
28 January 2019